blue zoo guides

bugs and
spiders

by Dee Phillips

Published in North America in 2006 by Two-Can Publishing
11571 K-Tel Drive, Minnetonka, MN 55343
www.two-canpublishing.com

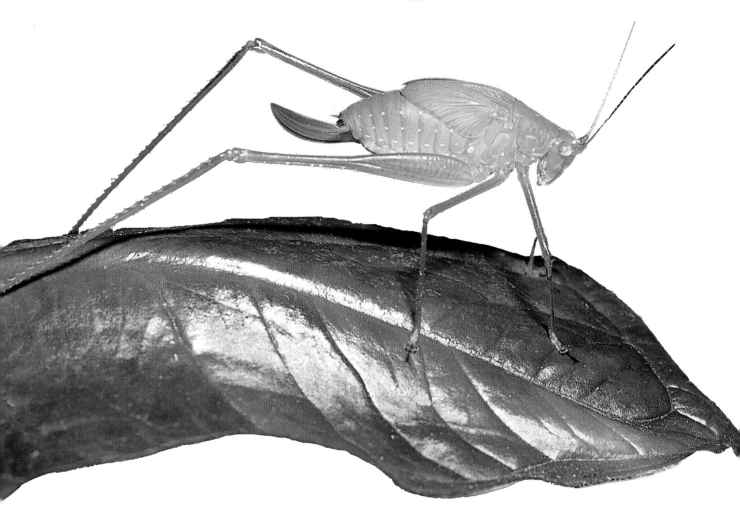

Copyright © ticktock Entertainment Ltd 2006
First published in Great Britain in 2006 by ticktock Media Ltd.,
Unit 2, Orchard Business Centre, North Farm Road, Tunbridge Wells, Kent, TN2 3XF

Library of Congress Cataloging-in Publication Data

Phillips, Dee, 1967-
Bugs and spiders / by Dee Phillips.
p. cm. -- (Blue zoo guides)
Summary: "Introduces insects, spiders, and other invertebrates from around the world, including information
about where they live, what they eat, and how they grow and survive"--Provided by publisher.
Includes index.
ISBN 1-58728-520-7 (reinforced hardcover)
1. Insects--Juvenile literature. 2. Spiders--Juvenile literature. I. Title. II. Series.
QL467.2.P54 2006
595.7--dc22   2005018824

1 2 3 4 5 10 09 08 07 06
Printed in China

Contents

Words that appear in **bold** are explained in the glossary.

A Buggy World

Did you know that there are more than a MILLION kinds of bugs living all over the world? By bugs, we're talking about ants, bees, beetles, butterflies, spiders, centipedes, and a whole lot of other little creatures that creep and flutter and skitter and buzz around us.

All of these bugs are **invertebrates**—animals without backbones. Leeches, slugs, and snails are also invertebrates, so we've decided to include them in this book, too. Are you ready to meet some of the coolest members of this buggy world of ours? Then turn the page!

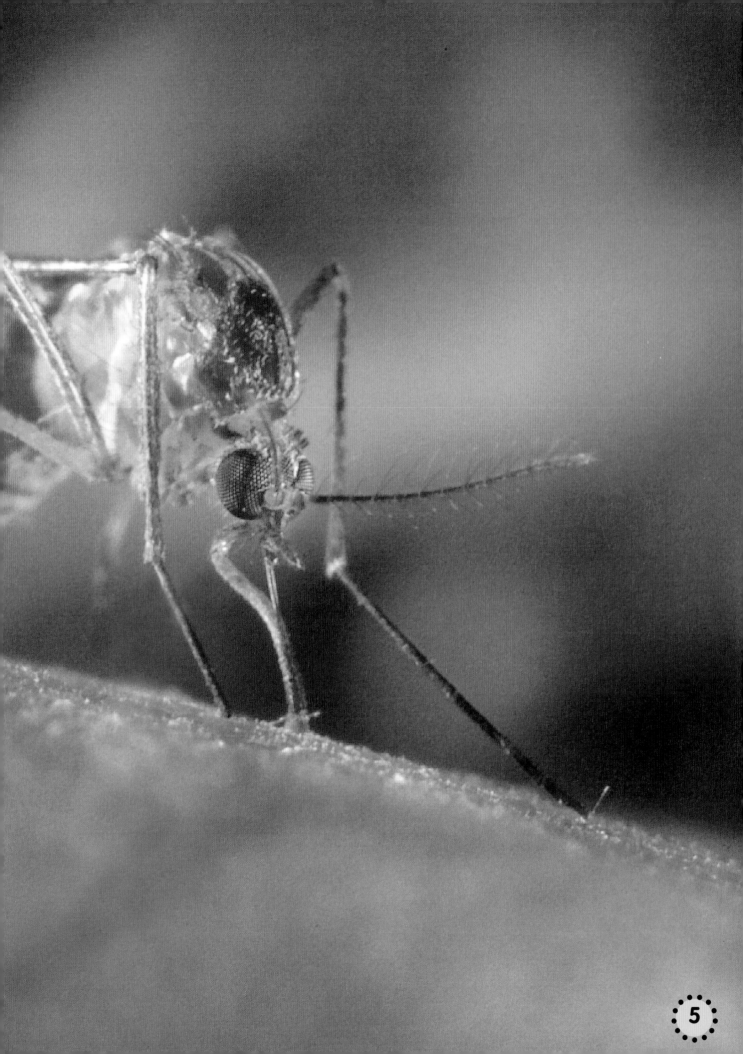

Bug Basics

Most of the creatures we call bugs (or invertebrates) belong to the insect family. All insects have two important things in common. They have six legs, and their bodies have three parts: the **head,** the **thorax,** and the **abdomen.** Many have wings, but some do not.

Spiders and scorpions are not insects. They all have eight legs and no wings. Centipedes and millipedes have even more legs. And slugs, snails, and leeches have no legs at all.

Except for scorpions, all of the bugs in this book start out life as an egg. But once the eggs hatch, things get more complicated. The young of some insects are called larvae (say "LAR-vee"). Just one of them is called a **larva** (LAR-vuh). Larvae look very different than their parents. Their bodies go through big changes before they become adults. Other insect young are called **nymphs** (NIMFS). They look more like small adults. On each page of this book, look for the big arrows to read about how each kind of bug grows up.

Ant

Ants can live almost anywhere. There are thousands of different kinds. Ants eat tiny insects and sweet drinks such as **nectar** and **honeydew.** They feel around with two pointy **antennae.**

An ant's abdomen is made up of a narrow waist section and a bigger part called the **gaster.**

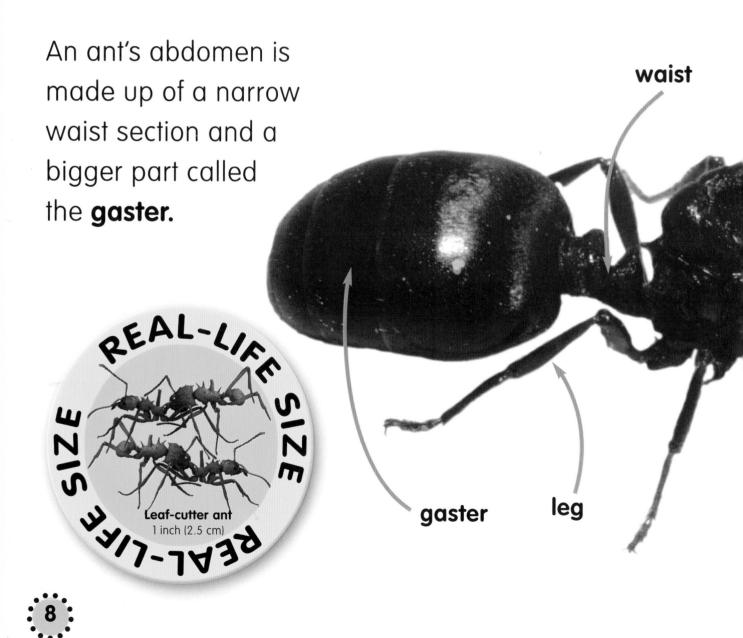

waist

REAL-LIFE SIZE
REAL-LIFE SIZE

Leaf-cutter ant
1 inch (2.5 cm)

gaster   leg

Ants live in a group called a **colony.** One or more queen ants lay all the eggs. Female workers raise the young and find food. Only queens and males have wings.

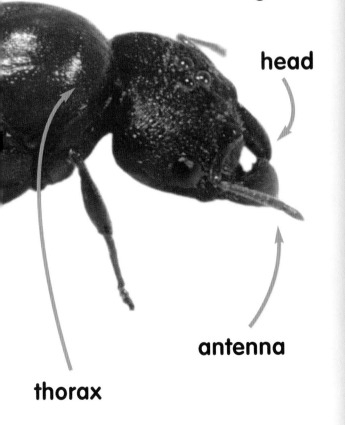

head

antenna

thorax

Ant Life Cycle

The queen ant lays an egg.

A larva hatches from the egg.

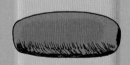

The larva grows and changes into a **pupa.**

An ant hatches from the pupa.

Aphid

Aphids are small, soft-bodied insects that live on plants. They feed on **sap** from young leaves. There are many different kinds of aphids.

Aphids produce a sugary waste called honeydew. This sweet liquid is a tasty food for ants, bees, and wasps.

antenna

head

abdomen

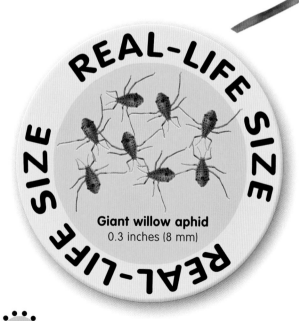

REAL-LIFE SIZE
REAL-LIFE SIZE

Giant willow aphid
0.3 inches (8 mm)

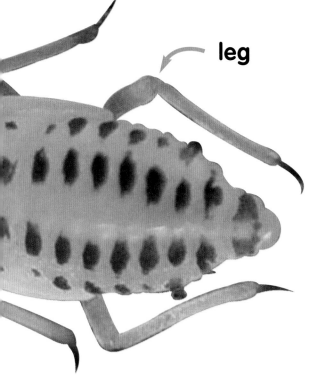

leg

Aphid Life Cycle

A female aphid lays an egg.

A wingless female aphid hatches from the egg.

The aphid grows up and lays eggs that produce more wingless females.

In the autumn, a wingless female lays eggs that hatch into winged male and female aphids.

Aphids live and feed together in colonies. These colonies are sometimes guarded by ants, who eat the aphids' honeydew.

Army Ant

Army ants travel in huge colonies. They eat everything that they can find and kill, including scorpions, beetles, and grasshoppers. They use long jaws called **mandibles** to sting them.

Army ants have tiny eyes, but they cannot see. They use their antennae to smell, touch, and communicate.

eye

REAL-LIFE SIZE
REAL-LIFE SIZE

Dorylus wilverthi
queen
2 inches (5 cm)

mandible

antenna

Army ants are always traveling. To make a quick nest, they grab each other's jaws and claws to form a ball around the queen and her eggs.

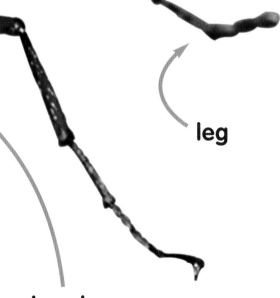

leg

head

Army Ant Life Cycle

The queen ant lays an egg.

A larva hatches from the egg.

The larva grows and changes into a pupa.

An ant hatches from the pupa.

Bedbug

Bedbugs are small, flat insects. They get their name from their favorite place to live: beds! They are **parasites** that bite animals and feed on their blood.

A bedbug bite looks like a line of tiny bumps on the victim's skin.

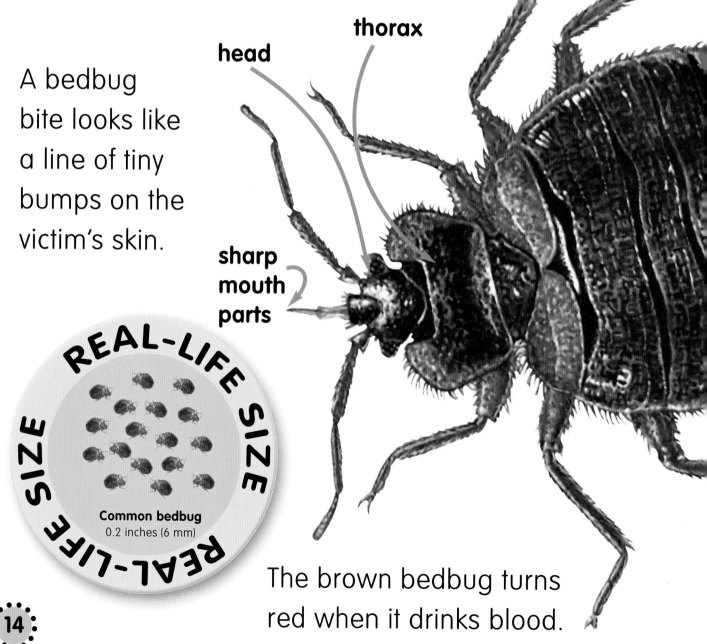

head

thorax

sharp mouth parts

REAL-LIFE SIZE
REAL-LIFE SIZE

Common bedbug
0.2 inches (6 mm)

The brown bedbug turns red when it drinks blood.

Bedbugs hide during the day and come out at night to look for food.

abdomen

leg

Bedbug Life Cycle

The female bedbug lays an egg.

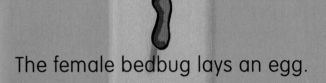

A nymph hatches from the egg.

The nymph passes through five growth stages.

The nymph becomes an adult bedbug.

Butterfly

Butterflies are winged insects that live for only a short time. They have a mouth shaped like a straw. This is handy for sucking nectar from flowers.

There are thousands of different kinds of butterflies. They have two pairs of colorful wings.

antennae

abdomen

hind wing

How **BIG** is a **butterfly?**

12 inches (30 cm)

0.6 inches
(15 mm)

Smallest:
Western
pygmy blue

Largest:
Queen
Alexandra's
birdwing

forewing

The wings of the leaf butterfly below look just like real leaves! Its ability to blend into its surroundings is called **camouflage.**

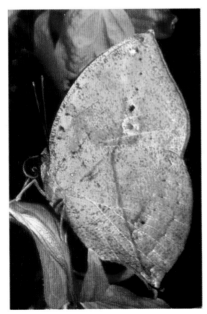

Butterfly Life Cycle

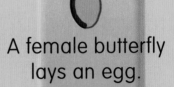

A female butterfly lays an egg.

A larva called a caterpillar hatches from the egg.

The larva grows up and turns into a pupa, or chrysalis.

The pupa splits open, and a butterfly crawls out.

Caterpillar

Caterpillars are the larvae of butterflies and moths. They have very strong jaws for chewing leaves.

A young caterpillar spends most of its time eating and growing. Then it attaches itself to a twig and makes a hard outer shell called a pupa or a chrysalis.

sucker legs

How **BIG** is a **caterpillar?**

Smallest:
Sorrel pygmy moth larva
Largest:
Death's head hawk moth larva

0.08 inches (2 mm)

5 inches (12.5 cm)

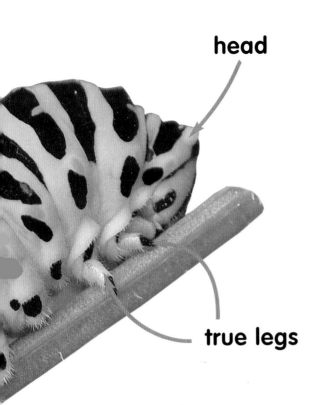

head

true legs

Caterpillars are eating machines. When a lot of caterpillars are eating together, you can actually hear munching noises!

Caterpillar Life Cycle

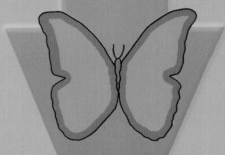

A female butterfly or moth lays an egg.

A caterpillar hatches from the egg.

The larva grows up and changes into a pupa, or chrysalis.

A butterfly or moth hatches from the pupa.

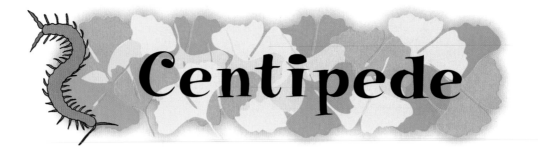

Centipede

Centipedes are fast-moving creatures with lots of legs. They eat insects, worms, spiders, slugs, and other small animals. They use poison to kill their **prey.**

The name centipede means "100 legs," but no centipede has exactly 100. Most have about 30 legs. But one kind has 254!

antenna

head

How **BIG** is a **centipede?**

0.4 inches (1 cm)

Smallest:
Hoffman's dwarf centipede

12 inches (30 cm)

Largest:
Giant Peruvian centipede

a body made up of many parts, called segments

Centipedes like to live in damp places under rocks and logs, or under piles of fallen leaves.

two legs on each segment

Centipede Life Cycle

A female centipede lays an egg.

A nymph hatches from the egg.

The nymph grows up to be an adult centipede.

Cicada

Cicadas are a kind of flying insect. Their **compound eyes** help them to see in many directions at once. Cicadas use their pointy jaws to suck sap from plants.

Male cicadas are noisy! In the summer, they sing a screechy song to attract a mate. They make the sound by moving small parts on their abdomen.

three legs on each side

How **BIG** is a **cicada?**

0.6 inches (14 mm)

Smallest: Dog day cicada

Largest: Giant cicada

8 inches (20 cm)

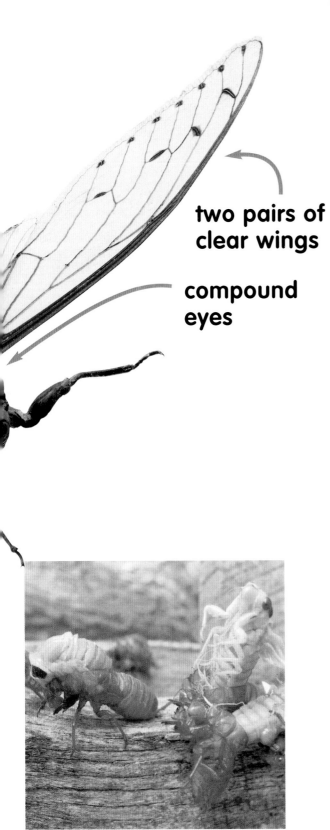

two pairs of clear wings

compound eyes

Cicadas spend up to 17 years underground. When they come out, they shed their skin to become adults.

Cicada Life Cycle

A female cicada lays an egg in the stem of a plant.

A nymph hatches from the egg. It drops to the ground and **burrows** into the soil. It sheds its old skin as it grows bigger.

The nymph digs its way out of the soil. It sheds its skin one last time to become an adult.

Cockroach

Cockroaches are insects. They are often found in places where food is stored or prepared. They eat almost anything, even paper and soap!

abdomen

Cockroaches can run fast. They hide in dark places during the day and come out at night to look for food.

How **BIG** is a **cockroach?**

Smallest:
Wheeler ant cockroach

Largest:
Borneo cockroach

0.2 inches
(4 mm)

4 inches (10 cm)

tiny hairs on legs help it to feel its surroundings

A cockroach has two points called **cerci** at the end of its abdomen. The cerci are used to sense when danger is near.

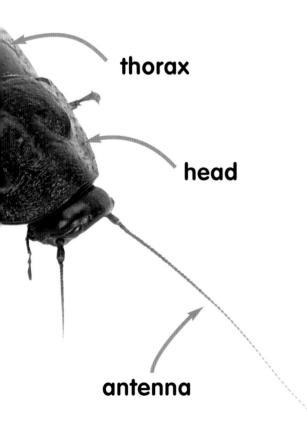

thorax

head

antenna

A female cockroach lays eggs.

A wingless nymph hatches from the egg.

The nymph grows up to be an adult cockroach.

Dragonfly

Dragonflies are insects with beautiful, **transparent** wings. There are about 5,000 different kinds. They are all strong fliers that can stop and **hover** in one place.

A dragonfly nymph lives underwater. An adult lives on land (and in the air!) near water.

large eyes

head

long, thin abdomen

How **BIG** is a **dragonfly?**

0.6 inches (15 mm)

6.3 inches (16 cm)

Smallest: Pygmy dragonfly

Largest: Australian giant dragonfly

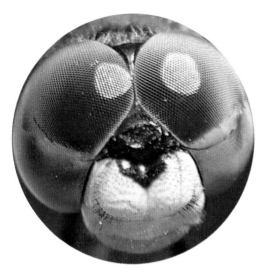

A dragonfly's large compound eyes cover most of its head. They help it catch its dinner: other flying insects!

forewing

hind wing

Dragonfly Life Cycle

A female dragonfly lays an egg in or near water.

A nymph hatches from the egg.

The nymph grows up to be an adult dragonfly.

Dung Beetle

Dung beetles come out at night. Different kinds of dung beetles eat the dung of different animals. These helpful beetles keep the planet clean and our soil healthy.

Dung beetles use their strong front legs to dig tunnels and burrows.

hard wing cases

six hairy legs

How **BIG** is a **dung beetle?**

0.1 inches (3 mm)

Smallest:
Ciervo aegialian scarab

Largest:
Elephant dung beetle

2.5 inches (6 cm)

Some female dung beetles lay their eggs in a ball of dung to keep them safe. When the larvae hatch, they have food waiting for them!

thorax

head

antenna

Dung Beetle Life Cycle

A female dung beetle lays an egg.

A larva hatches from the egg.

The larva changes into a pupa.

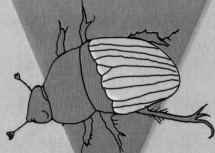

A adult dung beetle comes out of the pupa.

Earwig

Earwigs are insects. Some earwigs have wings, and other do not. They eat dead or live insects, as well as plants. Female earwigs guard their eggs from **predators.**

The earwig got its name because people used to believe that it crawled into their ears when they were asleep. But they don't really do that.

legs

pincers for grabbing prey

REAL-LIFE SIZE
REAL-LIFE SIZE

Saint Helena earwig

3 inches (8 cm)

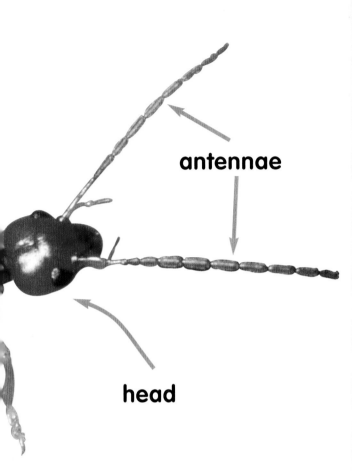

antennae

head

Female earwigs are good mothers. They watch over their eggs and lick them clean until the eggs hatch.

Earwig Life Cycle

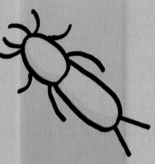

A female earwig lays an egg.

A nymph hatches from the egg.

The nymph grows up to be an adult earwig.

Firefly

Fireflies are winged beetles. Most kinds of fireflies can make the end of their abdomen light up. They flash this light at night to attract a mate.

Fireflies eat other insects, slugs, and snails. Sometimes they even eat other fireflies.

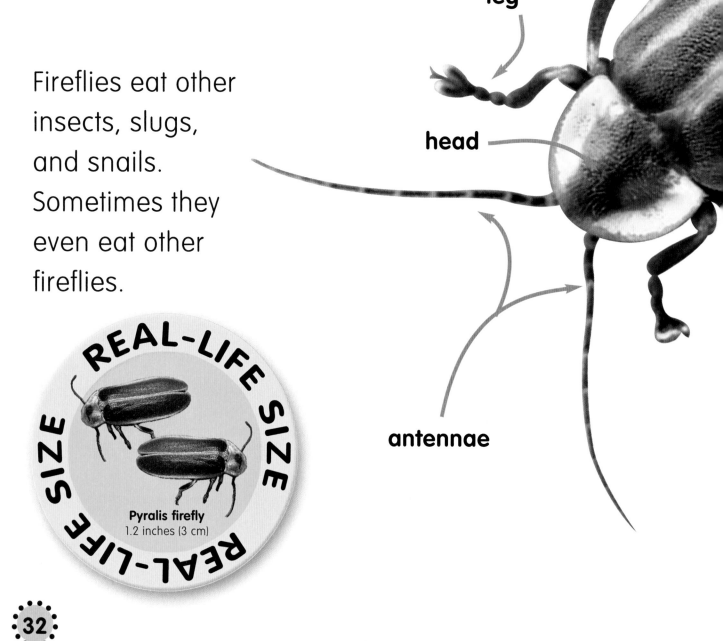

leg

head

antennae

REAL-LIFE SIZE
REAL-LIFE SIZE

Pyralis firefly
1.2 inches (3 cm)

wing case

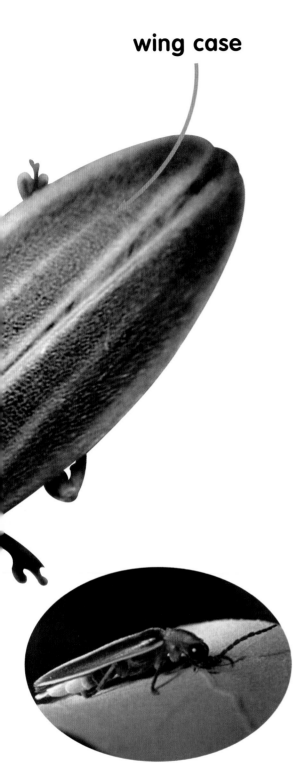

Like many beetles, the firefly has hard **wing cases** that close over its thin wings when the insect is not flying.

Firefly Life Cycle

A female firefly lays an egg.

A larva hatches from the egg.

The larva grows up and changes into a pupa.

An adult firefly hatches from the pupa.

Flea

Fleas are insects called parasites. They live on people or animals and feed on their blood.

Each kind of flea lives on a different kind of **host,** such as cats or dogs. Fleas use their sharp mouth parts to bite through skin.

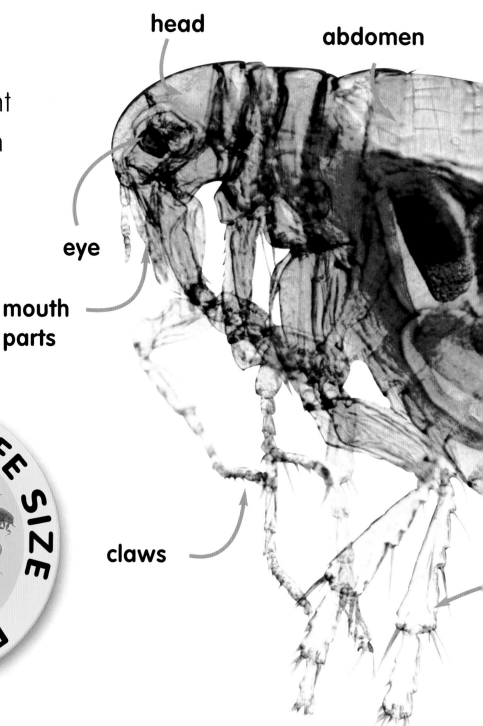

head

abdomen

eye

mouth parts

claws

REAL-LIFE SIZE

Mountain beaver flea
0.3 inches (8 mm)

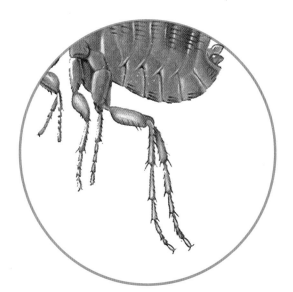

A tiny flea has powerful back legs. It can leap as far as 6 inches (15 cm) to land on a host animal.

long back legs

Flea Life Cycle

A female flea lays an egg.

A larva hatches from the egg.

The larva grows up and changes into a pupa.

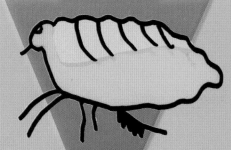

An adult flea comes out of the pupa.

Fly

Flies are very good at . . . flying! They can beat their wings 200 times a second. Many flies use their **saliva** to turn fruit and other plant material into liquid food. Other flies eat insects or drink blood.

Flies have tiny hooks and sticky pads on their feet to grip the places they land. They can even hang upside down!

abdomen

one pair of transparent wings

leg

How **BIG** is a **fly?**

Smallest:
Long-legged fly

Largest:
Giant robber fly

0.04 inches
(1 mm)

2.8 inches (7 cm)

Flies taste their food with hairs on their feet.

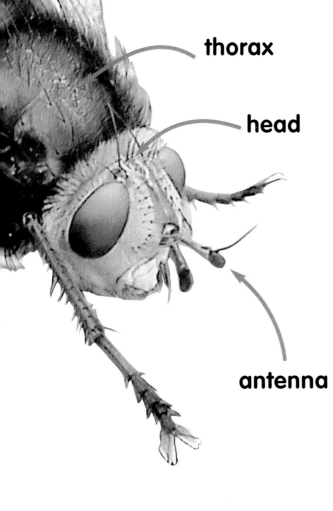

thorax

head

antenna

Fly Life Cycle

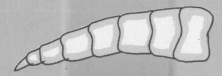

The female fly lays an egg.

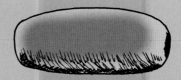

A larva, or maggot, hatches from the egg.

The larva grows up and turns into a pupa.

The pupa splits open and an adult fly comes out.

Giant Millipede

The giant millipede is an invertebrate with LOTS of legs. Most kinds of millipedes have between 100 and 300 legs. The most leggy millipede has 750! The giant millipede eats dead plants and rotting wood.

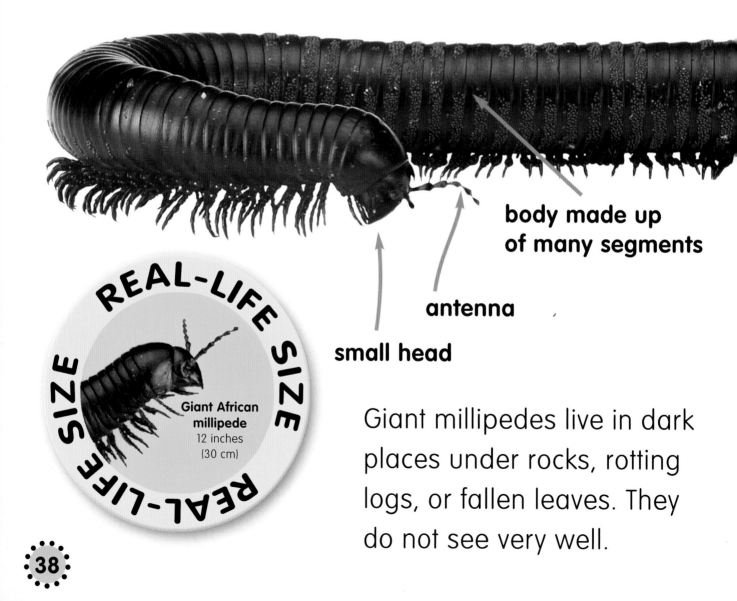

body made up of many segments

antenna

small head

REAL-LIFE SIZE

REAL-LIFE SIZE

Giant African millipede
12 inches
(30 cm)

Giant millipedes live in dark places under rocks, rotting logs, or fallen leaves. They do not see very well.

If a millipede senses danger, it curls up so that its head and soft underside are protected.

four legs on each body segment

Giant Millipede Life Cycle

A female millipede lays an egg.

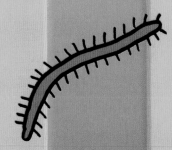

A young millipede hatches from the egg.

The young millipede grows up to be an adult.

Grasshopper

Grasshoppers are a group of insects that are excellent jumpers. Locusts are part of this group. Grasshoppers eat grasses and other plants.

Male grasshoppers rub their back legs against their leathery wings to make a loud, chirping sound. This sound attracts female grasshoppers.

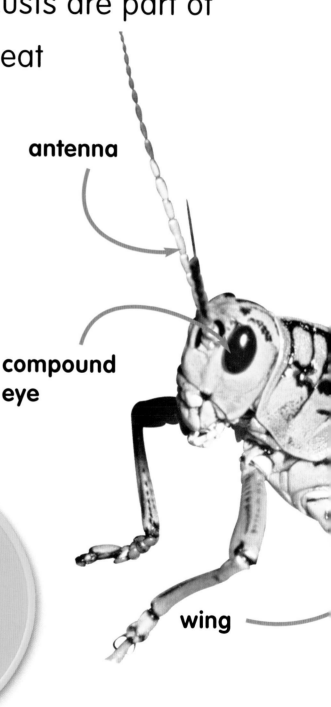

antenna

compound eye

wing

How **BIG** is a **grasshopper?**

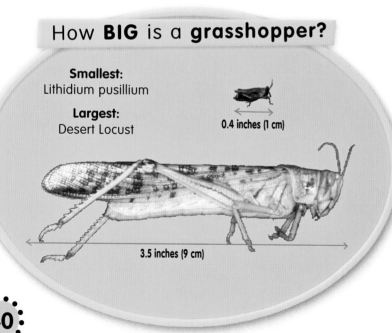

Smallest:
Lithidium pusillium

Largest:
Desert Locust

0.4 inches (1 cm)

3.5 inches (9 cm)

To escape danger, a grasshopper may choose to jump rather than fly away. It has strong back legs.

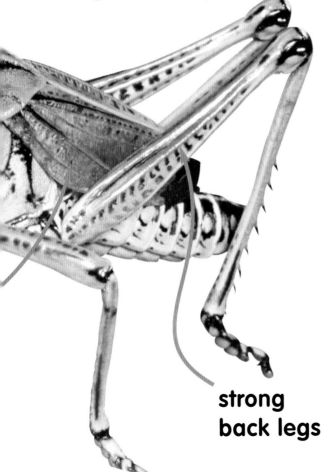

strong back legs

Grasshopper Life Cycle

A female grasshopper lays an egg.

A nymph hatches from the egg.

The nymph grows up to be an adult grasshopper.

Ground Beetle

Ground beetles are just one of many, many different kinds of beetle. They eat insects and small, soft bodied animals, including worms and fly larvae.

Ground beetles do their hunting at night. During the day, they hide under logs or rocks, or in narrow cracks in the ground.

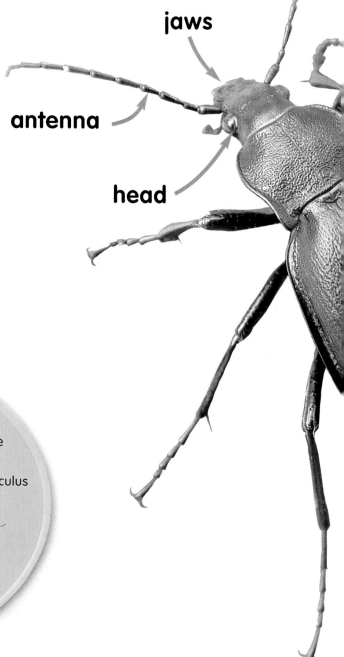

jaws

antenna

head

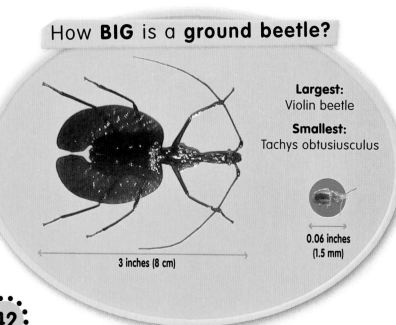

How **BIG** is a **ground beetle?**

Largest:
Violin beetle

Smallest:
Tachys obtusiusculus

0.06 inches
(1.5 mm)

3 inches (8 cm)

Some ground beetles have colorful wing cases that sparkle like jewels.

wing cases

leg

Ground Beetle Life Cycle

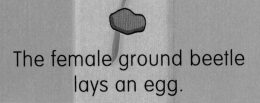

The female ground beetle lays an egg.

A larva hatches from the egg.

The larva grows up and changes into a pupa.

An adult ground beetle comes out of the pupa.

Head Louse

A head louse is a small, wingless insect. It is a parasite that feeds on human blood. Head lice lay their eggs in the victim's hair!

Head lice have flat bodies. Their front legs have hook-like claws to grab on to the hairs on a person's head and neck.

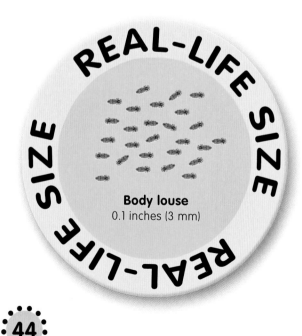

REAL-LIFE SIZE
REAL-LIFE SIZE

Body louse
0.1 inches (3 mm)

abdomen

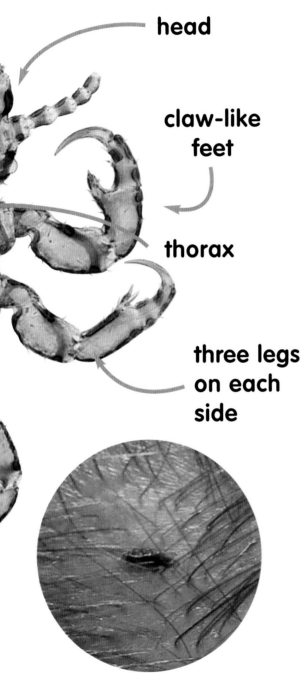

head

claw-like feet

thorax

three legs on each side

Head lice love clean human hair. They spread by jumping from head to head!

Head Louse Life Cycle

A female head louse lays an egg called a nit.

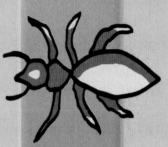

A nymph hatches from the egg.

The nymph grows up to be an adult head louse.

Honeybee

Honeybees spend much of their time collecting nectar and **pollen** from flowers. They eat some and use the rest to make honey. The bees eat honey when flowers are not blooming.

Honeybees live in a group called a **colony.** Their home is called a hive.

one pair of wings

abdomen

baskets on the back legs for carrying pollen

REAL-LIFE SIZE
REAL-LIFE SIZE

Giant honeybee
0.7 inches (19 mm)

compound eye

thorax

Worker bees clean the hive, make honey, and care for the colony's young.

Honeybee Life Cycle

The queen bee lays an egg.

A larva hatches from the egg.

The larva grows and changes into a pupa.

The pupa splits open, and an adult honeybee crawls out.

Jumping Spider

Jumping spiders are a group of small, hairy spiders. Some are brightly colored. They have eight legs. They also have eight eyes! Jumping spiders eat insects.

The jumping spider can see its prey from up to 12 inches (30 cm) away. It sneaks up on its victim, then jumps on it. Its bite is deadly.

abdomen

leg

REAL-LIFE SIZE
REAL-LIFE SIZE

Green jumping spider
0.5 inches (12 mm)

A jumping spider can jump a long way for such a small spider. It leaps on to its prey before the insect can see it coming.

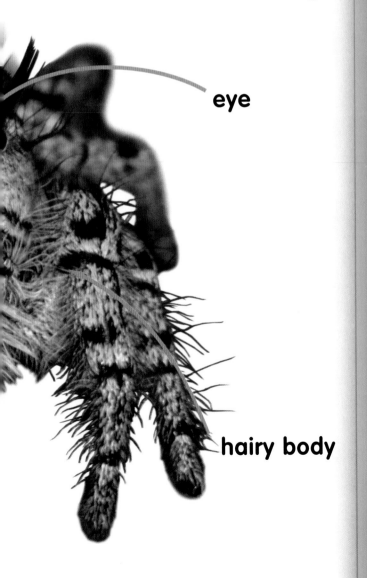

eye

hairy body

Jumping Spider Life Cycle

A jumping spider lays an egg.

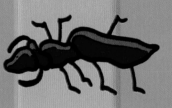

A spiderling hatches from the egg.

The spiderling grows up to be an adult.

Ladybug

Ladybugs are a kind of beetle. They help protect gardens by eating tiny pests called aphids.

Ladybugs have hard wing cases to protect their wings. The bright color tells birds, "I taste bad. Don't eat me!"

REAL-LIFE SIZE

Seven-spotted lady beetle
0.3 inches (7 mm)

wings fold up when not in use

hard wing case

leg

antenna

head

When it is cold, ladybugs huddle together to keep warm. During the winter, they **hibernate** under logs, leaves, or bark.

Ladybug Life Cycle

A female ladybug lays an egg.

A larva hatches from an egg.

The larva grows and changes into a pupa.

Inside the pupa, the ladybug develops into an adult.

Leafhopper

Leafhoppers are small insects that cause a lot of damage to plants. There are thousands of different kinds. They feed on trees, grasses, and farm crops.

The mouth of a leafhopper is shaped like a straw. It pierces the leaves of plants and sucks out the sap.

eye

thorax

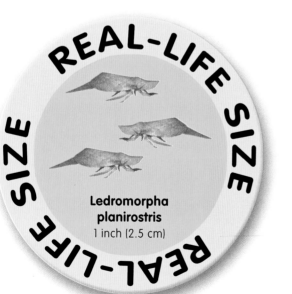

REAL-LIFE SIZE

Ledromorpha
planirostris
1 inch (2.5 cm)

52

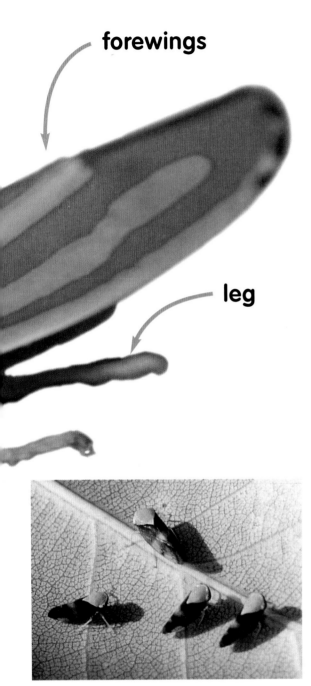

forewings

leg

Leafhoppers make sounds to communicate with other leafhoppers. Humans cannot hear these sounds.

Leafhopper Life Cycle

A female leafhopper lays an egg.

A nymph hatches from the egg.

The nymph grows up to be an adult leafhopper.

Leeches are a kind of worm. Different kinds of leeches feed on the blood of different kinds of animals. Many kinds of leeches live in fresh water. Others live on land.

A leech's body is made up of many segments, or sections. It has a small mouth at one end. Some kinds have two eyes. Others have as many as ten!

sucker

How **BIG** is a **leech?**

7 inches (18 cm)

0.2 inches (5 mm)

Smallest:
Acanthobdella
peledina

Largest:
Americobdella
valdiviana

sucker → ← mouth

head

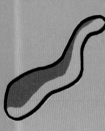

A leech has a **sucker** at each end of its body. These suckers help it to move and to hold on while it feeds.

Leech Life Cycle

A female leech lays an egg.

A young leech hatches from the egg.

The young leech grows into an adult leech.

Locust

Locusts are a kind of grasshopper. They eat many kinds of plants and can cause a lot of damage to crops.

Locusts have very strong back legs. They can jump up to ten times their own length. They also have long wings for flying.

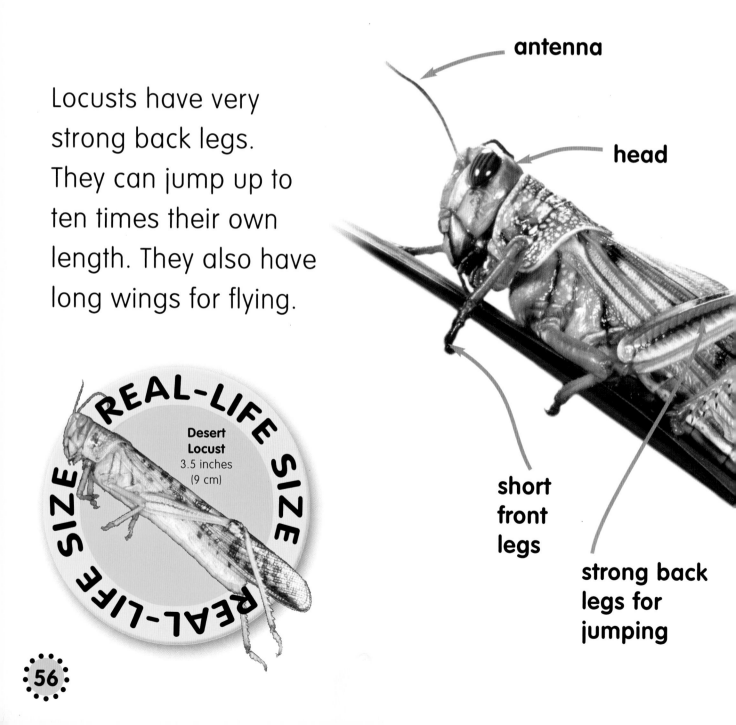

antenna

head

short front legs

strong back legs for jumping

REAL-LIFE SIZE
REAL-LIFE SIZE

Desert Locust
3.5 inches
(9 cm)

Locusts travel together in a huge group called a swarm. They can gobble up an entire farm field very quickly.

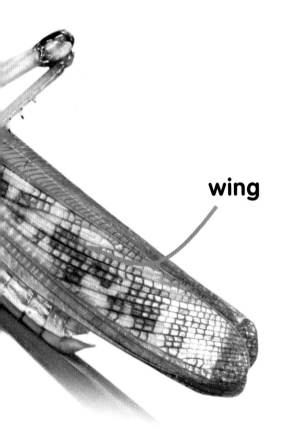

wing

Locust Life Cycle

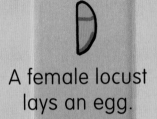

A female locust lays an egg.

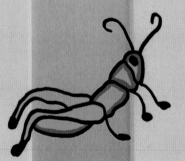

A nymph hatches from the egg.

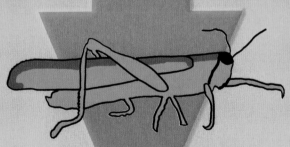

The nymph grows up to be an adult locust.

Longhorn Beetle

Longhorn beetles are a group of insects that are known for their long antennae. Longhorn larvae eat wood and can cause major damage to trees.

A longhorn beetle's antennae are often longer than its body!

leg

wing cases

How **BIG** is a **longhorn beetle?**

Smallest:
Purpuricenus humeralis

Largest:
Giant longhorn beetle

3.5 inches (9 cm)

0.2 inches (5 mm)

Some longhorn beetles have wasp-like markings to scare off predators.

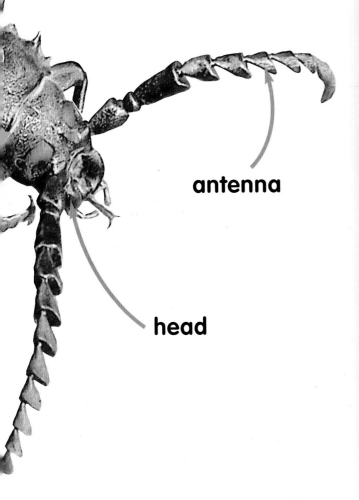

antenna

head

Longhorn Beetle Life Cycle

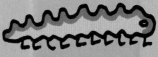
The female beetle lays an egg.

A larva hatches from the egg.

The larva grows up and changes into a pupa.

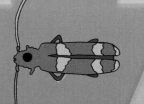
A beetle hatches from the pupa.

Mole Cricket

Mole crickets live in underground burrows. They use their strong front legs for digging. Some kinds eat only roots and plants. Others also eat worms and larvae.

Male mole crickets make a chirping sound by rubbing their wings together.

head

large eyes

broad front legs

REAL-LIFE SIZE REAL-LIFE SIZE

Prairie mole cricket
2 inches (5 cm)

longer back legs

Female mole crickets stay in their burrows to protect their nymphs.

Mole Cricket Life Cycle

A female cricket lays an egg.

A nymph hatches from the egg.

The nymph grows up to be an adult cricket.

Mosquito

Mosquitoes are flies. There are about 2,000 different kinds. The females feed on animal blood. The males eat nectar.

two wings

The mosquito has a sharp, tube-shaped mouth. The female uses the tube to poke through an animal's skin and suck up its blood. The victim may feel itchy afterward.

abdomen

three legs on each side

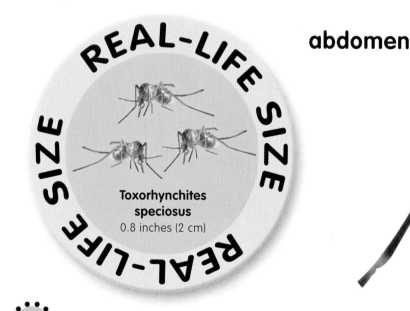

REAL-LIFE SIZE

REAL-LIFE SIZE

Toxorhynchites speciosus
0.8 inches (2 cm)

antenna

mouth

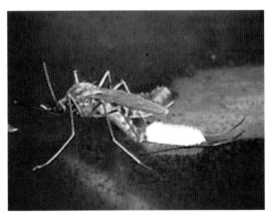

Female mosquitoes lay their eggs on the surface of water.

Mosquito Life Cycle

A female mosquito lays an egg on the surface of water.

A larva hatches from the egg and drops into the water.

The larva grows up underwater and changes into a pupa.

An adult mosquito hatches from the pupa and flies away.

Moth

Moths are winged insects. Most kinds of moths are active at night. They eat nectar from flowers.

Unlike butterflies, most moths have feathery antennae and wings that are not very colorful.

antenna

head

abdomen

hind wing

How **BIG** is a **moth?**

12 inches (30 cm)

Smallest: Enteucha acetosae

Largest: Atlas moth

0.1 inches (3 mm)

forewing

Moths often lay their eggs on the underside of a leaf.

Moth Life Cycle

A female moth lays an egg.

A larva hatches from the egg.

The larva grows and changes into a pupa.

Inside the pupa, the larva changes into an adult moth.

Praying Mantis

Praying mantises, or mantids, belong to the cockroach family. Their large eyes help them spot their prey. They eat other insects, such as beetles and butterflies.

A praying mantis whips out its spiky front legs to grab other insects. The spikes help it hold its wiggling prey while the mantis starts eating!

head

antenna

spiky front legs

How **BIG** is a **praying mantis?**

Smallest:
Bolbe pygmaea

Largest:
Large brown mantid

7 inches (18 cm)

0.3 inches (8 mm)

When a praying mantis is about to grab a meal, it holds its front legs up as if it were praying.

abdomen

Praying Mantis Life Cycle

A female praying mantis lays an egg.

A nymph hatches from the egg.

The nymph grows into an adult praying mantis.

Raft Spider

Raft spiders are also known as fishing spiders. They stand on the water and grab insects, tadpoles, and even small fish. Like all spiders, they have two body parts: the **cephalothorax** and the abdomen.

A female raft spider spins a web like a tent to hold her eggs.

cephalothorax

REAL-LIFE SIZE
REAL-LIFE SIZE

Fen raft spider
1 inch (2.5 cm)

Hairs on the spider's legs help it feel slight movements in the water. This way, it can tell if food is nearby!

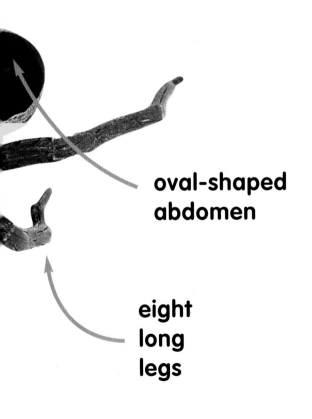

oval-shaped abdomen

eight long legs

Raft Spider Life Cycle

A female raft spider lays eggs.

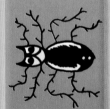

A spiderling hatches from an egg.

The spiderling grows up to be an adult raft spider.

Rhinoceros Beetle

Rhinoceros beetles have large horns. They live in forests. The adults eat rotting fruit and sap. The larvae eat wood.

A rhinoceros beetle often uses its horns like shovels. It digs a burrow to escape from danger. Male beetles also use their horns to fight.

three strong horns

spiky legs

How **BIG** is a **rhino beetle?**

Smallest:
Allomyrina
pfeifferi

Largest:
Megasoma
actaeon

4.7 inches (12 cm)

1.6 inches (4 cm)

Rhinoceros beetles are very strong. They can carry loads up to 850 times their own weight.

hard wing cases

Rhino Beetle Life Cycle

A female rhinoceros beetle lays an egg.

A larva hatches from the egg.

The larva grows and changes into a pupa.

An adult rhinoceros beetle comes out of the pupa.

Scorpion

Scorpions are related to spiders. They have eight legs, plus two strong claws for grabbing their prey. They eat insects and small animals.

Scorpions rest under rocks during the day and hunt at night. A female scorpion carries her babies on her back to keep them safe.

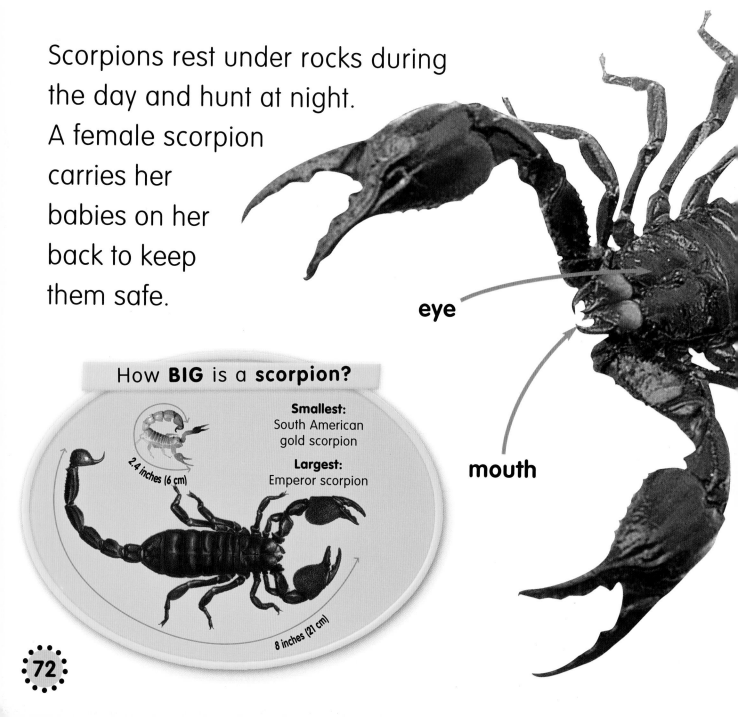

eye

mouth

How **BIG** is a **scorpion?**

2.4 inches (6 cm)

Smallest:
South American gold scorpion

Largest:
Emperor scorpion

8 inches (21 cm)

A scorpion has a stinger
at the tip of its tail.
The sharp point sends
deadly poison into
the victim's body.

stinger

eight legs

Scorpion Life Cycle

A female scorpion gives birth
to a live young scorpion.

The young scorpion grows
up to be an adult scorpion.

Slug

Slugs are part of the **mollusk** family. Mollusks live in or near water and have soft bodies. Slugs live on land. They eat **fungi** and rotting plants.

A slug is like a snail without a shell. It moves by squeezing muscles on the underside of its body. It leaves a trail of slime wherever it goes!

body covered in slippery slime

How **BIG** is a **slug?**

0.7 inches
(18 mm)

Smallest:
Gray garden slug

Largest:
Ash-black slug

12 inches (30 cm)

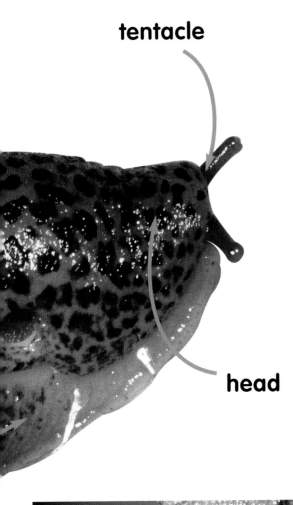

tentacle

head

A slug has a soft, moist body that dries out quickly. It hides in damp places and comes out only at night or when it is wet.

Slug Life Cycle

A female slug lays an egg.

A nymph hatches from the egg.

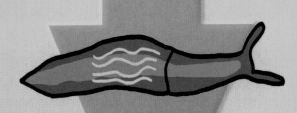

The nymph grows into an adult slug.

Snail

Snails are a lot like slugs, but they have hard shells. Snails that live on land eat plants. Some snails that live in ponds and oceans also eat live or dead animals.

A snail has a soft body that is protected by a hard shell. When the snail senses danger, it pulls its body inside the shell.

hard spiral shell

soft body

How **BIG** is a **land snail?**

Smallest:
Ammonicera rota

Largest:
Giant African land snail

0.04 inches (1 mm)

12 inches (30 cm)

eye

two large and two small tentacles

In dry weather, a land snail can seal up the opening of its shell to keep from drying out.

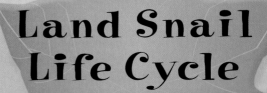

Land Snail Life Cycle

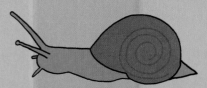

A female snail lays an egg.

A young snail hatches from the egg.

The young snail grows into an adult snail.

Stag Beetle

Stag beetles are fierce-looking beetles. They live under logs and tree stumps. The larvae eat rotting wood and roots. The adults eat tree sap.

A male stag beetle has enormous jaws that look like antlers. The beetle uses them to fight other males. Stag beetles also have wings.

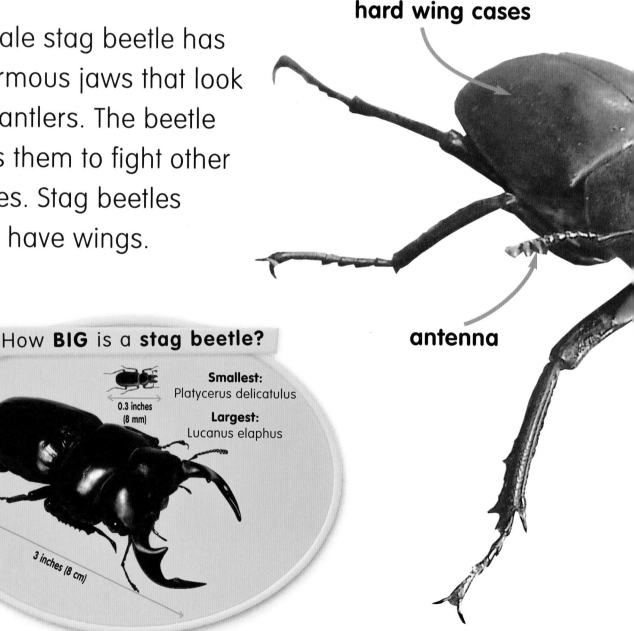

hard wing cases

antenna

How **BIG** is a **stag beetle?**

0.3 inches (8 mm)

Smallest:
Platycerus delicatulus

Largest:
Lucanus elaphus

3 inches (8 cm)

Male stag beetles are much bigger than the females.

thorax

head

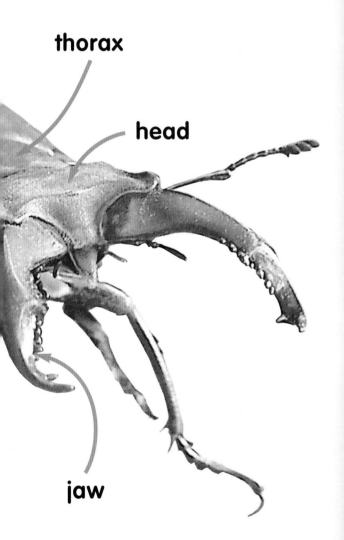

jaw

Stag Beetle Life Cycle

A female beetle lays an egg.

A larva hatches from the egg.

The larva grows and changes into a pupa.

The pupa splits open and an adult stag beetle comes out.

Stick Insect

There are about 2,000 kinds of stick insects. They use camouflage to hide from hungry birds. From the air, they look just like sticks! Stick insects wait until dark to move around and feed on leaves.

Some stick insects can make their own leg fall off if a predator grabs it. This gives the insect a chance to escape. The leg grows back later.

abdomen

six long, thin legs

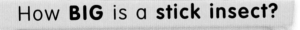

How **BIG** is a **stick insect?**

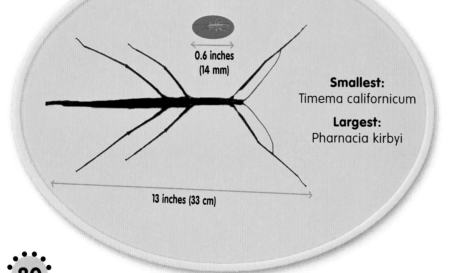

0.6 inches
(14 mm)

Smallest:
Timema californicum

Largest:
Pharnacia kirbyi

13 inches (33 cm)

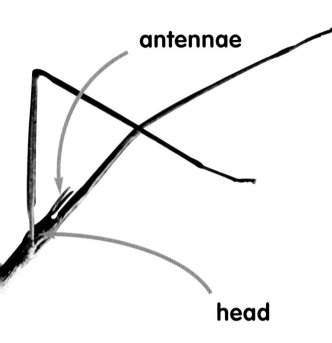

antennae

head

Some stick insects are covered with sharp points called spines. This helps them to hide in prickly bushes.

Stick Insect Life Cycle

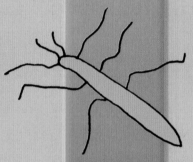

A female stick insect lays an egg.

A nymph hatches from the egg.

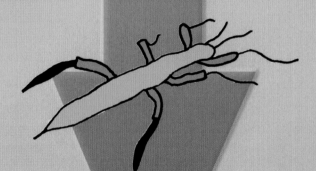

The nymph grows up to be an adult stick insect.

Stinkbug

Stinkbugs are insects that are often found in farm fields. They feed on whatever crops they can find, such as corn and beans.

Stinkbugs come in many different colors. They can spray a stinky liquid to keep predators away.

antenna

narrow head

body shaped like a shield

REAL-LIFE SIZE

Predatory stinkbug
0.8 inches (2 cm)

A stinkbug called the parent bug guards her eggs and cares for the nymphs after they hatch.

tough forewings that close over thin hind wings

Stinkbug Life Cycle

A female stinkbug lays an egg.

A nymph hatches from the egg.

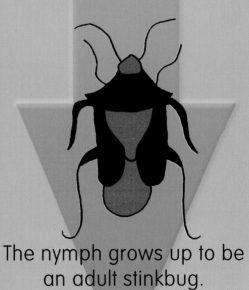

The nymph grows up to be an adult stinkbug.

Tarantula

Tarantulas are hairy spiders. Most are very large. They use sharp **fangs** to kill insects, lizards, frogs, small birds, and even snakes.

Tarantulas have a deadly bite that sends poison into their prey.

abdomen

strong jaws

one of two pedipalps, used to hold on to prey

How **BIG** is a **tarantula?**

0.2 inches (5 mm)

Smallest:
Spruce fir moss spider

Largest:
Goliath tarantula

11 inches (28 cm)

Tarantulas often live in underground burrows. They come out at night to hunt.

eight hairy legs

Tarantula Life Cycle

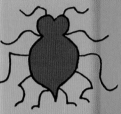

A female spider lays an egg.

A spiderling hatches from the egg.

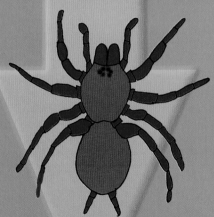

The spiderling grows into an adult tarantula.

Termite

Termites are insects that live in large colonies. The nests of some kinds of termites are tall towers of soil. Others are papery balls high up in trees. Termites eat plants and wood.

Termites have soft bodies and rounded heads. Only the king and queen have wings.

queen termite

workers

REAL-LIFE SIZE
REAL-LIFE SIZE

Pacific dampwood termite
0.7 inches
(18 mm)

Worker termites have no wings. They build the nest and take care of the young. Soldier termites have strong jaws. Their job is to protect the nest.

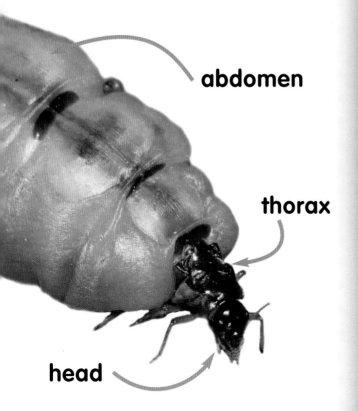

abdomen

thorax

head

Termite Life Cycle

The queen termite lays an egg.

A nymph hatches from the egg.

The nymph grows into an adult termite.

Tree Nymph

Tree nymphs are a type of butterfly. They are found mostly in rain forests. Like all butterflies, they sip liquid foods such as nectar.

The forewings of the tree nymph are almost twice as wide as they are tall. This makes them good fliers.

antenna

leg

small back wings

REAL-LIFE SIZE

Ceylon tree nymph

5 inches
(13 cm)

wide forewings

Male tree nymphs give off a scent, or smell, that attracts females.

Tree Nymph Life Cycle

A female tree nymph butterfly lays an egg.

A larva called a caterpillar hatches from the egg.

The larva changes into a pupa, or chrysalis.

A tree nymph butterfly comes out of the pupa.

Wasp

Wasps are a group of stinging insects. Some kinds live in colonies. Others live alone. Wasps like sweet foods such as fruit and nectar.

A worker wasp uses its stinger to **paralyze** caterpillars and other insects. They are used to feed the growing wasp larvae.

striped abdomen

transparent wings

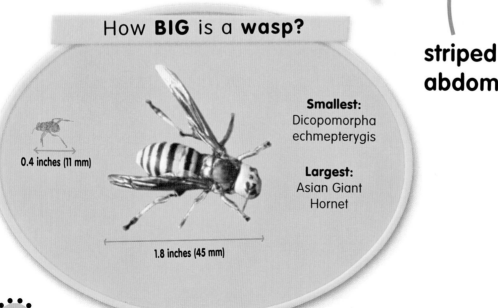

How **BIG** is a **wasp?**

0.4 inches (11 mm)

Smallest:
Dicopomorpha echmepterygis

Largest:
Asian Giant Hornet

1.8 inches (45 mm)

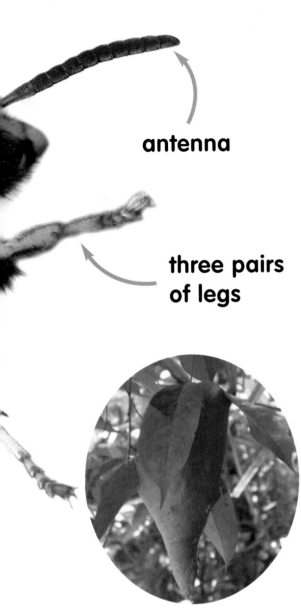

antenna

three pairs of legs

Some wasps make paper by chewing on wood. They use this paper to build their nests. A finished nest may have thousands of rooms!

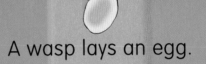

Wasp Life Cycle

A wasp lays an egg.

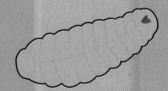

A larva hatches from the egg.

The larva changes into a pupa.

An adult wasp hatches from the pupa.

Wolf Spider

Wolf spiders hunt for their food and do not spin webs. They eat small animals and insects such as locusts and beetles. They usually hunt at night. Wolf spiders can see very well.

Wolf spiders have strong legs and can run very fast to catch their prey.

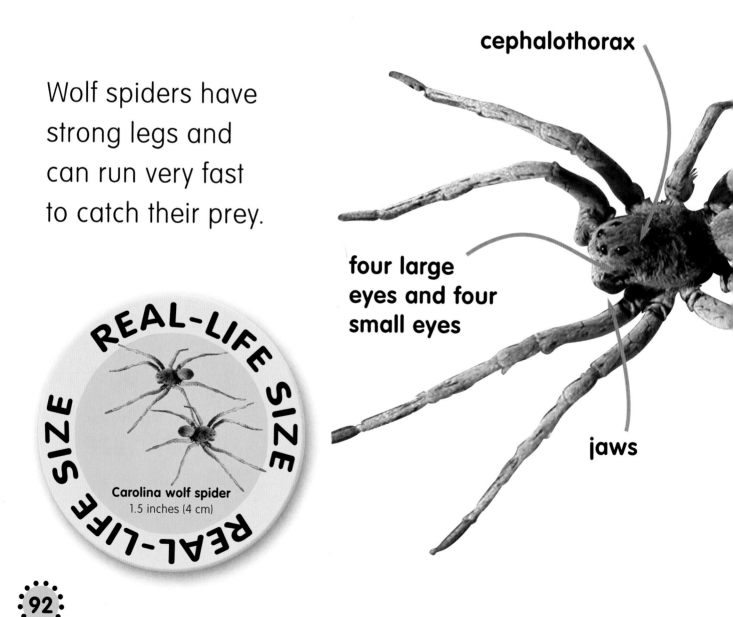

cephalothorax

four large eyes and four small eyes

jaws

REAL-LIFE SIZE
REAL-LIFE SIZE

Carolina wolf spider
1.5 inches (4 cm)

These spiderlings will live on their mother's back until they are big enough to hunt on their own.

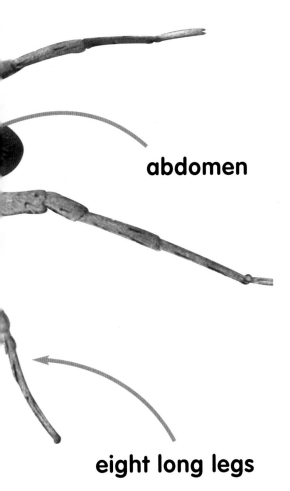

abdomen

eight long legs

Wolf Spider Life Cycle

A female spider lays an egg.

A spiderling hatches from the egg.

The spiderling grows into an adult wolf spider.

Glossary

abdomen: the bottom section of an insect's body

antenna: a long, thin feeler on an insect's head that is used for tasting and touching. **Antennae** means more than one.

burrow: to dig into the ground to hide or to live

camouflage: the ability to blend in with the colors of one's surroundings

cephalothorax: the front section of a spider, which includes the head and thorax

cerci: spikes at the end of an insect's abdomen that sense movement. One spike is called a **cercus.**

colony: a group of insects that live together and help each other survive

compound eye: an eye with many surfaces that lets an insect see in many directions at one time

fangs: large, sharp teeth used for biting into prey

forewings: the top pair of wings, closest to the head

fungi: plant-like living things such as mushrooms and molds

gaster: the main, rounded part of the abdomen in ants and bees

head: the front section of an insect, which contains the eyes, mouth parts, and antennae

hibernate: to spend the winter in a deep sleep

hind wings: the bottom pair of wings

honeydew: a sweet liquid produced by aphids

host: the animal upon which a parasite (such as a flea) lives and feeds

hover: to stop in the air while flying

invertebrates: animals that have no backbone, or spine. Invertebrates include insects, worms, mollusks, spiders, and shellfish such as lobsters

larva: the worm-like stage that some kinds of insects go through when they first hatch from an egg. A larva will change into a pupa before it becomes an adult. **Larvae** is the word for more than one larva.

mandibles: biting mouth parts of some insects

mollusks: a group of animals with soft bodies that includes snails, slugs, clams, and octopuses

nectar: a sweet liquid made by flowers that attracts insects and some birds

nymphs: the young of certain kinds of insects. They hatch from an egg looking like a smaller version of their parents.

paralyze: to make an animal unable to move

parasite: an animal that feeds on another animal without killing it

pincers: long claws of some bugs

pollen: yellow dust that a flower makes to help it produce new seeds

predator: an animal that eats other animals

prey: an animal that is food for other animals

pupa: the stage of some insects' lives between larva and adulthood. The insect goes through major changes while closed up in a shell or cocoon.

saliva: a liquid made by an animal's mouth

sap: the liquid inside a tree or other plant

sucker: a flat body part that allows an animal to cling to a surface

thorax: the middle section of an insect's body where the legs and wings attach

transparent: allowing light to pass through

wing cases: the hard front wings of beetles that fold over and protect the lower, flying wings

Index